LIGHT AND COLOUR

Design:
David West Children's Book Design
Designer: Edward Simkins
Editor:
Susannah Le Besque
Illustrator:
Tony Kenyon

Photography:
Roger Vlitos
apart from page 23:
with special thanks to
David Burder, 3-D Images
Models:
David Millea
Consultant:
Dr Bryson Gore

The publishers wish to point out that all the photographs reproduced in this book have either been posed by models or obtained from photographic agencies.

Created and produced by
NW Books
28 Percy Street
London W1P 9FF

First published in Great Britain in 1994 by
Watts Books
96 Leonard Street
London EC2A 4RH
ISBN 0 7496 1708 X

Printed in Belgium

SCIENCE FOR FUN

LIGHT AND COLOUR

GARY GIBSON

WATTS BOOKS
London • New York • Sydney

CONTENTS

INTRODUCTION

Have you ever wondered what would happen to the Earth if there were no sunlight? Did you know that light rays can bounce, bend and even be split into a rainbow? For centuries scientists worked to find out more about light and colour. This book contains a selection of exciting "hands-on" projects to help explain some of the fascinating discoveries that have been made about light and colour.

Whenever this symbol appears adult supervision is required.

LIGHT FOR LIFE

Green plants need sunlight to live and grow. They use the light's energy to grow. All animals get their food from plants, either directly or indirectly. Since plants need sunlight to grow, all living things depend on the sun.

GROWING CRESS

1 Put a layer of cotton wool in the bottom of two clean dishes. Dampen with a little water. Sprinkle cress seeds evenly over the cotton wool.

2 Put the dishes on a sunny window sill and cover each dish with a cardboard box. Make a hole in the side of one box and leave for several days. Check daily that the cotton wool is damp.

3 The seeds under the box with no hole have grown straight up looking for light. The cress under the box with the hole has grown toward the light.

WHY IT WORKS

Green plants contain a chemical called chlorophyll. Chlorophyll traps light which combines with water and air to help make the plant grow. This process is called "photosynthesis". Plants cannot see light but can bend and grow toward where it comes from.

FURTHER IDEAS

Follow step 1 again. Cover one dish with a large clean glass jar to make a "greenhouse". Compare the growing roots and shoots with the uncovered dish. Which seedlings grow the best?

DAY AND NIGHT

Half the world is in daylight and the other half in darkness. As the Earth spins around each part takes its turn to face the Sun. Parts of the Earth facing away from the Sun can be lit only by the moon. Sometimes the Moon passes between the Sun and the Earth, so the Sun's rays are blocked and the sky grows dark. This is called an eclipse.

MAKE A SUNDIAL

1 You need a piece of wood or thick card and a length of dowel. Make a hole near one edge of the wood for the dowel.

2 Stand the the dowel in the hole (fix with glue if necessary). Decorate using waterproof paints.

3 On a sunny morning put the sundial outside. The dowel casts a shadow; paint along the shadow.

4 Repeat step 3 every hour. Paint the time next to each shadow. The sundial will only work on sunny days. Remember to keep it in the same place facing the same way.

WHY IT WORKS

The stick blocks the Sun and casts a shadow. The shadow's position changes as the Sun moves across the sky.

As the Earth spins around, the Sun appears to move across the sky.

FURTHER IDEAS

Make a shadow animal with your hands. In a darkened room, get a friend to shine a torch onto the wall. Put your hands in front of the torch and see if you can make an animal-shaped shadow on the wall.

SEEING IMAGES

An image is a likeness of something or someone. What we see in photographs or a movie are images. A camera is a box that can make an image on photographic film. The film contains chemicals that will keep the image for years.

MAKE A PINHOLE CAMERA

1 Find a small cardboard box that does not let light through. Use a pair of scissors to cut away one side of the box.

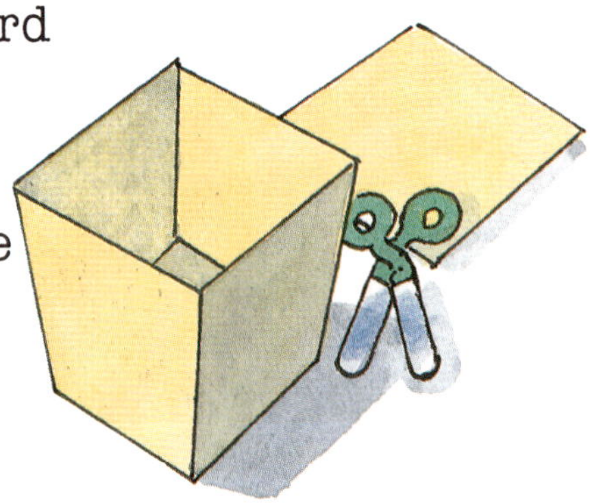

2 Tape a piece of tracing paper over the cut-away side of the box. Make sure that the tracing paper is kept as smooth as possible.

3 Make a pinhole in the side of the box opposite the tracing paper. Point the pinhole at a window. Move toward the window until you see its image on the tracing paper.

WHY IT WORKS

Light rays in air do not bend or curve, they always travel in straight lines. Rays of light from the window enter the pinhole in straight lines and hit the tracing paper. The light rays from the bottom and the top of the window cross over as they pass through the hole, so the image appears upside down.

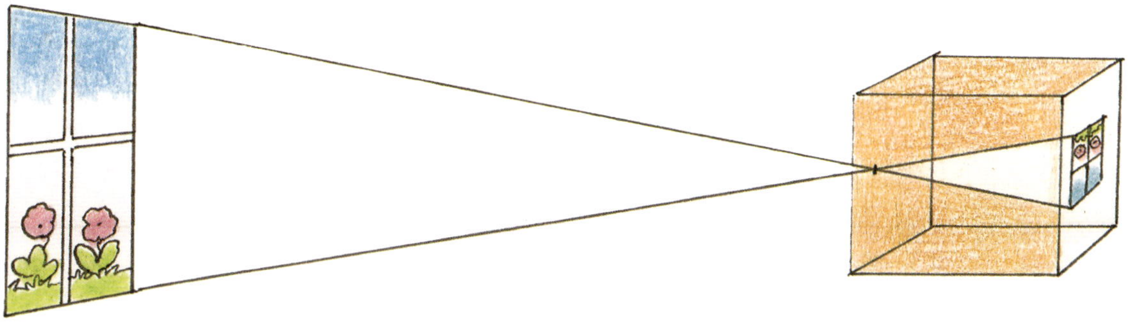

FURTHER IDEAS
Make the pinhole a little bigger so more light enters the camera. The image becomes brighter but less clear. A magnifying glass in front of the pinhole can sharpen the image. The image will be faint so point the pinhole at a bright object such as a light bulb.

BOUNCING LIGHT

Rays of light can be bounced off an object like a rubber ball bouncing off a wall. We call this "reflection". Light rays are reflected best by flat, shiny surfaces such as shiny spoons, tins, bottles or mirrors.

MAKE A KALEIDOSCOPE

1 Carefully tape together three identical-sized small mirrors. Make a triangle- shaped tube with the shiny sides facing inside.

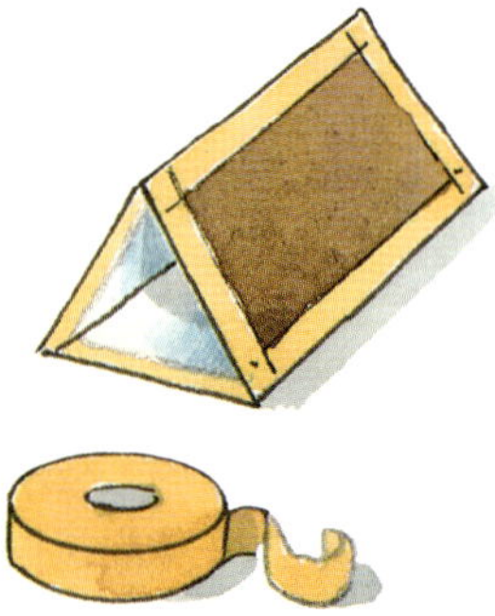

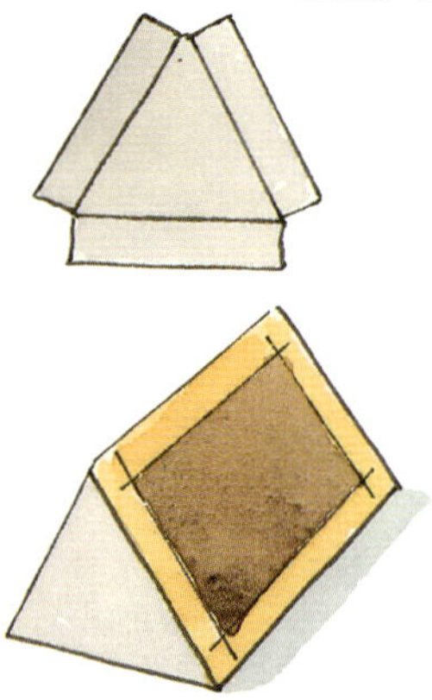

2 Cut out a triangle-shaped piece of paper, allowing for flaps. Tape it over one end of the triangle of mirrors to form a box.

3 Cut out small pieces of brightly coloured paper from a magazine and drop them into the bottom of the box.

4 Tape another triangle of paper over the other end of the tube. Using a pencil, make a hole to look through. The kaleidoscope is finished.

5 Hold the kaleidoscope level, point it at a bright light. Look at the pattern through the eye piece. Shake and look again.

WHY IT WORKS

Light rays from the coloured paper are reflected back and forth between the mirrors. Each image is doubled by the mirrors before the light rays reach your eye.

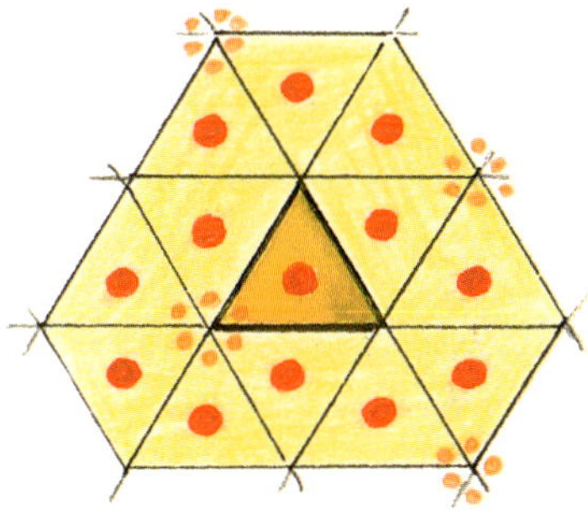

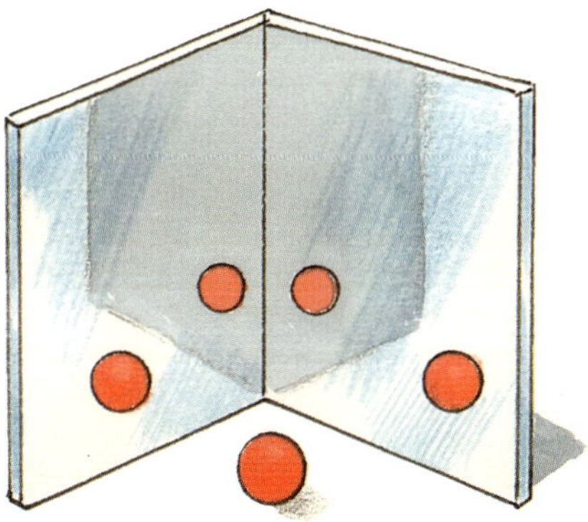

FURTHER IDEAS
Stand two mirrors up at right-angles with modelling clay. Place a marble between the mirrors. How many images can you see?

UP PERISCOPE!

Submarine crews want to know what is going on above the waves without being seen. Instead of rising to the ocean's surface, the submarine raises its periscope. On land you can use periscopes to see over walls and round corners!

MAKE A PERISCOPE

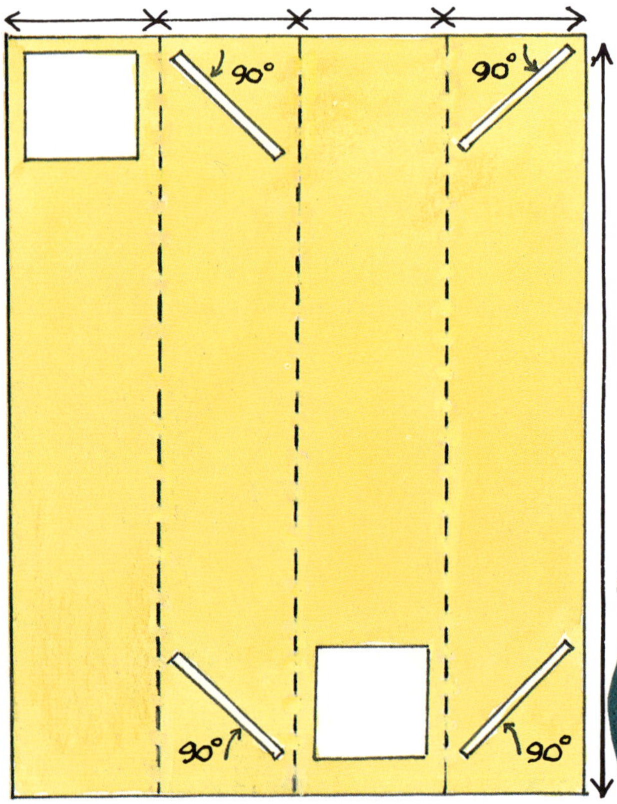

1 Copy the pattern above onto card. Cut around the outline. Cut out the slots and squares. Fold on the dotted lines.

2 Tape the edges of the card together to form a box. Make sure that the slots line up. Paint to decorate.

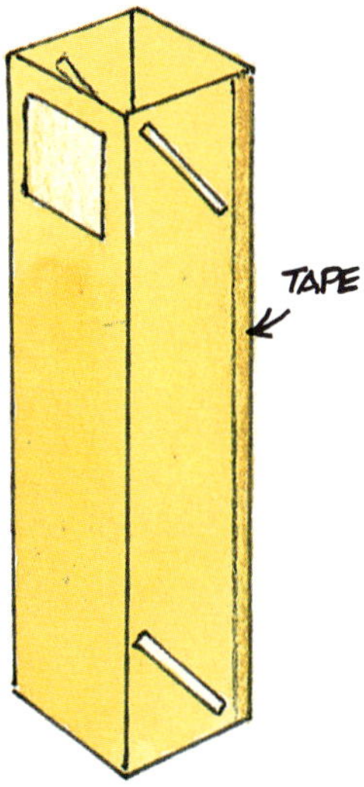

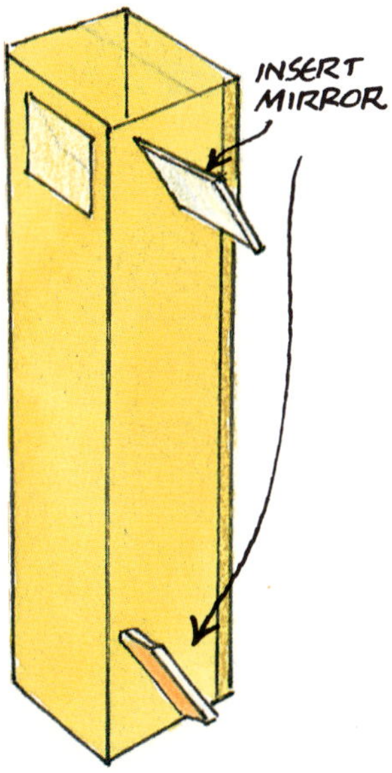

3 Insert two mirrors into the slots, top mirror facing down, bottom mirror facing up. Look into the lower mirror.

WHY IT WORKS

Light rays above and ahead of you hit the upper mirror. It reflects the rays down to the lower mirror which in turn reflects the light rays into your eyes.

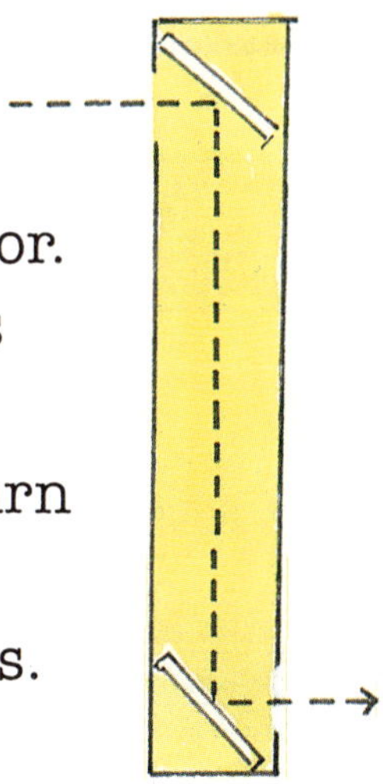

FURTHER IDEAS

Make a periscope to see around corners. Copy the design shown below. Follow instructions 1 and 2 as before. But this time the angles of the mirror slots are different. Make sure the top mirror faces down and the bottom mirror faces up.

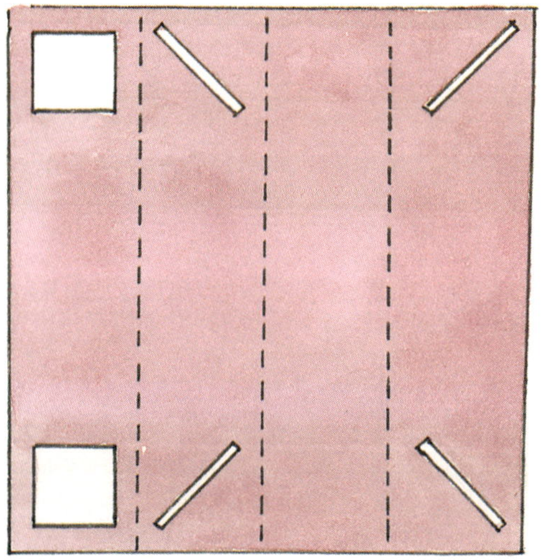

MOVING PICTURES

Cartoon films are made out of many drawings. These are photographed one after another by a movie camera. When the film is projected onto a screen the images seem to move. If you move your eyes quickly over the pictures on the right, the ball seems to bounce.

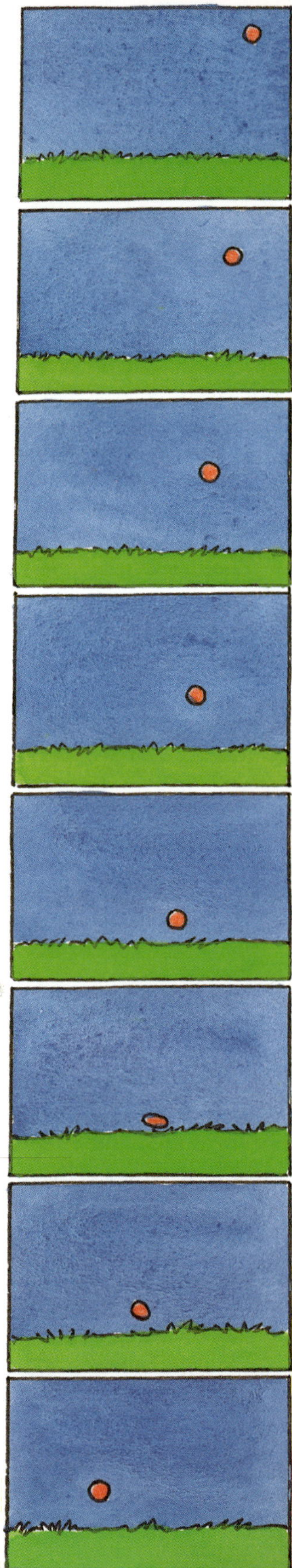

MAKE A FLICK BOOK

1 Draw a background picture. Trace it onto at least twelve pages of the same size. Leave a margin down one side of each drawing.

2 Draw the Sun high in the sky on the first page. Draw it slightly lower on the second page. Repeat until the Sun has set on the last page.

3 Stack the pages neatly and staple them together with two staples along the edge of the margin.

WHY IT WORKS

Your eyes see each image for a fraction of a second. If the images are shown fast enough the eye runs the images together. Differences in the separate images appear as movement.

FURTHER IDEAS

Copy the two faces (below) onto two sheets of tracing paper. Staple the two sheets together. Roll the upper sheet tightly around a pencil. Move the pencil up and down to roll and unroll the upper sheet.

4 Hold the flick book by the margin and watch the Sun go down as you flick the pages.

SPLITTING LIGHT

300 years ago Sir Isaac Newton proved that white light is made from the colours of the rainbow. Newton split white light into a rainbow using a wedge of glass called a prism. We see rainbows in the sky because water droplets in the air split the sunlight before it reaches us.

MAKE A RAINBOW

1 Get an adult to cut a slit in a piece of black card. Shine a lamp through the slit and ensure you get a narrow beam of light.

2 Angle a mirror in a bowl of water. Slope a large piece of white card away from the bowl.

3 Shine a light through the slit in the black card and onto the mirror. Adjust both pieces of card until you get the best rainbow.

4 You should be able to see all seven colours of the rainbow.

WHY IT WORKS

When a beam of light is shone into glass or water, it bends. Each of the colours in white light bends at a slightly different angle. This causes the colours to split apart. Each colour reflected from the mirror becomes spread out on the screen.

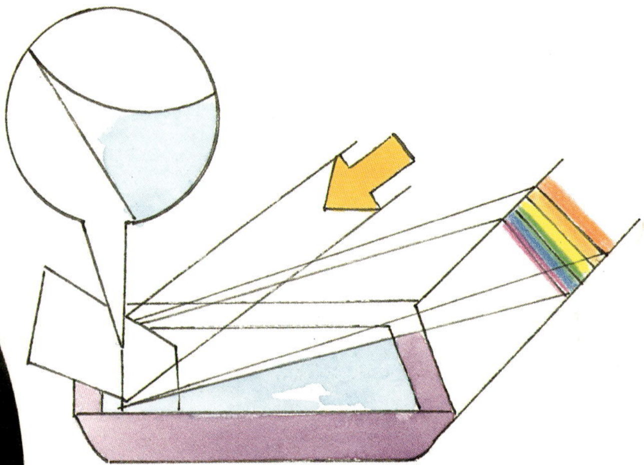

FURTHER IDEAS

Shine a torch at an angle onto a long-playing record or compact disc. Each of these objects can split light into a rainbow.

MIXING COLOURS

Look closely at a colour TV or the photographs in this book. The pictures are made up of lots of tiny coloured dots. Because we see books or TV from a distance, the dots seem to mix to make colours.

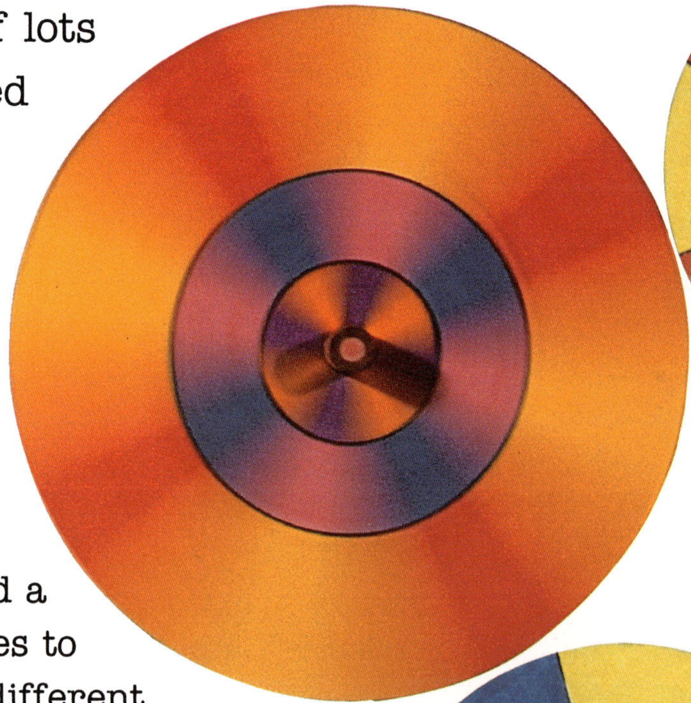

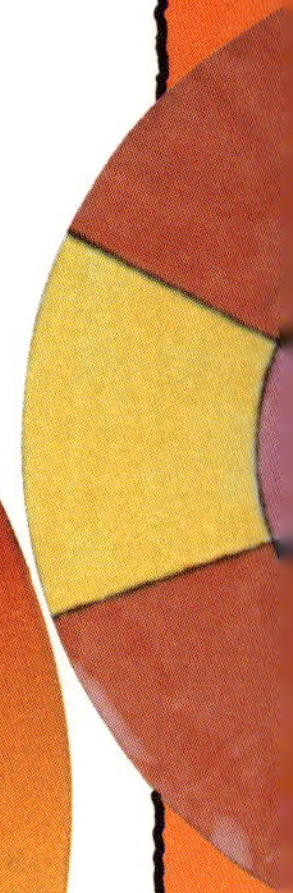

MAKE A COLOUR SPINNER

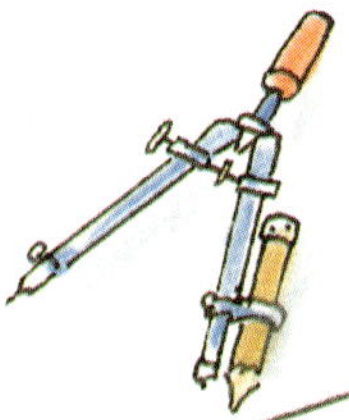

1 Use a pencil and a pair of compasses to draw circles of different sizes onto white card. Cut them out with scissors.

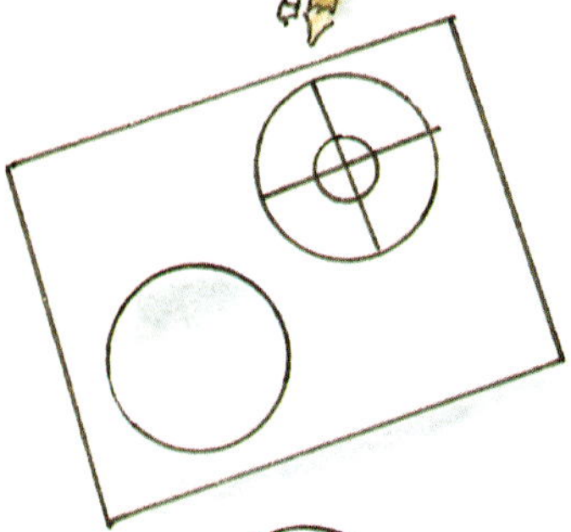

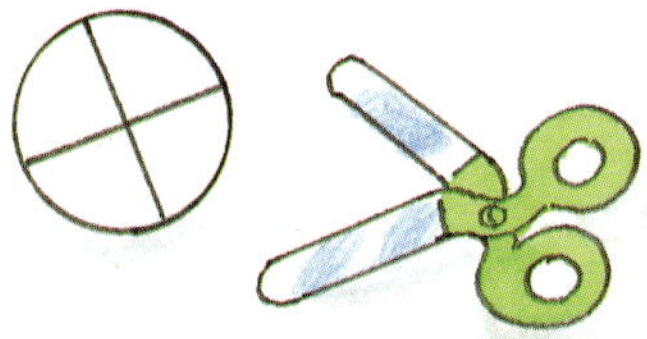

2 Divide the circles into equal sections and decorate each section with different colours. Push a sharp pencil or stick through the hole in the centre of each circle.

3 Spin the the spinner as fast as you can on a table top and watch the different colours merge. If you colour a spinner with the colours of the rainbow, when you spin it, it may appear white.

WHY IT WORKS

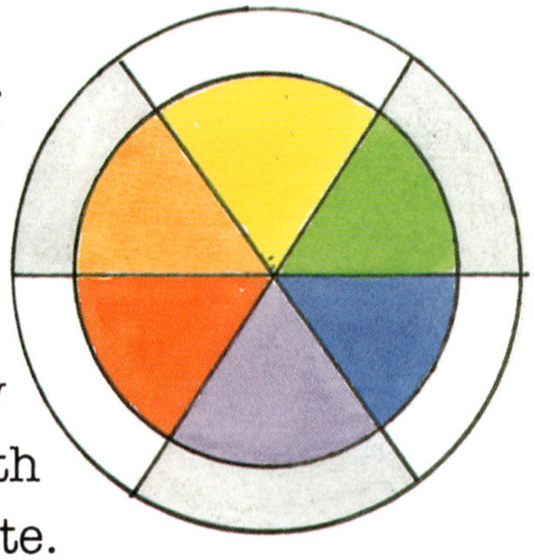

The spinner is turning so fast that instead of seeing separate colours, our eyes see a mixture. White light is made up of the colours of the rainbow so a spinner decorated with these colours appears white.

FURTHER IDEAS

Cover three torches with red, blue, and green cellophane. Shine them onto white paper (or a white floor). Allow the light beams to overlap. See how many new colours you can make.

SEEING IN THREE DIMENSIONS

Animals usually have two eyes. Close one eye and look at an object. Guess how far away it is. Try again with both eyes open. It is much harder to judge distances using only one eye. Having two eyes gives us a sense of depth.

MAKE 3D GLASSES

1 Measure the distances A and B around your head with a paper tape measure.

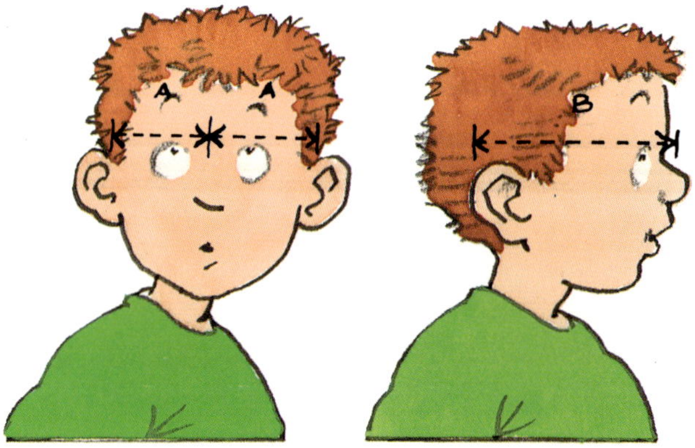

2 Use the distances to draw out your glasses onto card. Cut out the glasses and fold along the dotted lines.

3 Cut out red and green cellophane for the eyeholes. Glue the green over the right eyehole and red over the left. Try on the glasses. Look at the insect picture opposite.

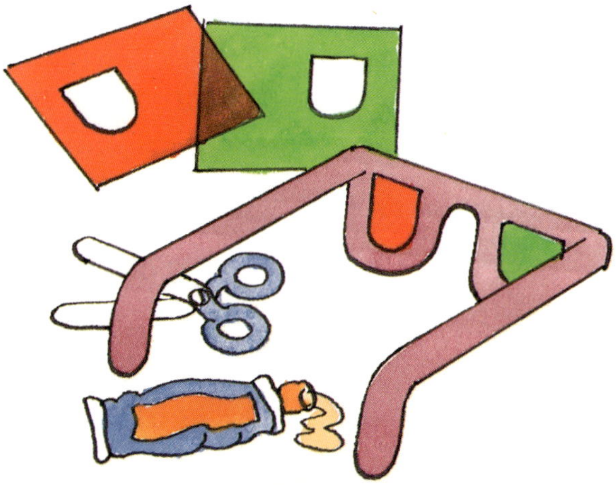

WHY IT WORKS

The left eye covered with red cellophane only sees the green image; the right eye only sees the red. Each eye sees a different view. The brain combines both images to give the illusion of depth.

FURTHER IDEAS

Close one eye. Hold your hands out in front of you at arm's length. Bring your index fingers together so they touch. Can you thread a needle with one eye closed?

SEPARATING COLOURS

In printing and painting there are three primary colours – red, blue, and yellow. The enormous variety of coloured dyes, paints and inks are made by mixing different amounts of two or more of the primary colours.

FIND THE HIDDEN COLOURS

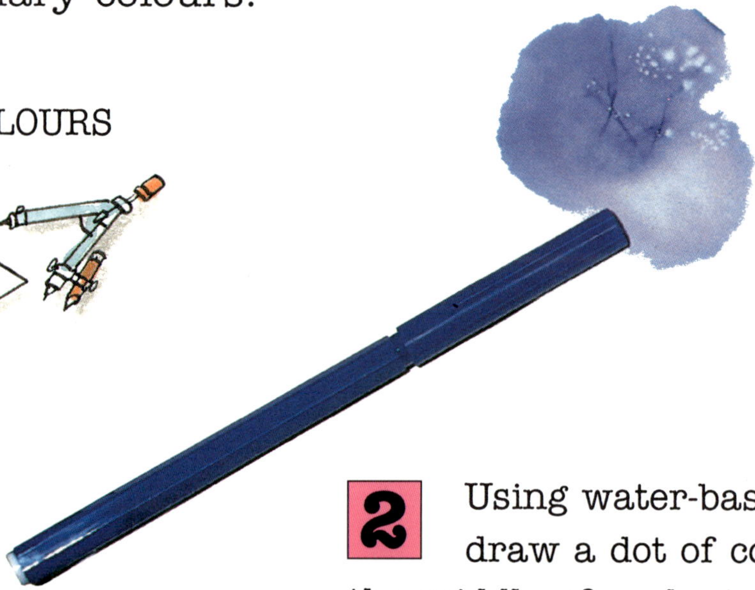

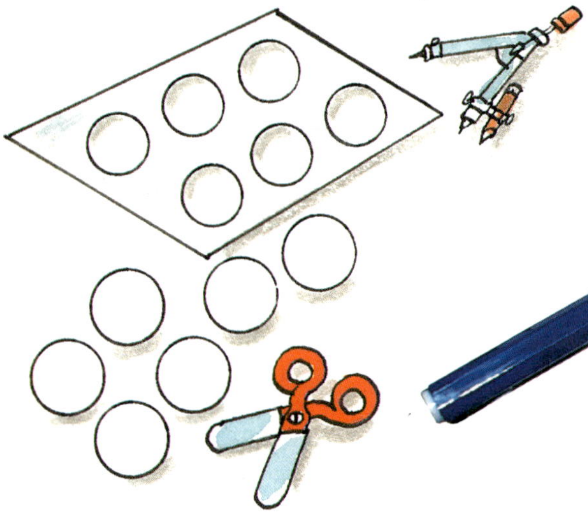

1 With a pair of compasses draw some circles onto blotting paper. Cut them out with scissors.

2 Using water-based pens draw a dot of colour in the middle of each circle. Black, purple, green, brown, and orange are good colours to use.

3 Place each circle of blotting paper over the top of a clean, dry jar.

4 Add drops of water to the dot of colour. Dip a straw into water. Block the top with your finger. Touch the ink dot with the straw.

WHY IT WORKS

Some inks are made up of several colours. These can separate as the water spreads, carrying the colours at different speeds.

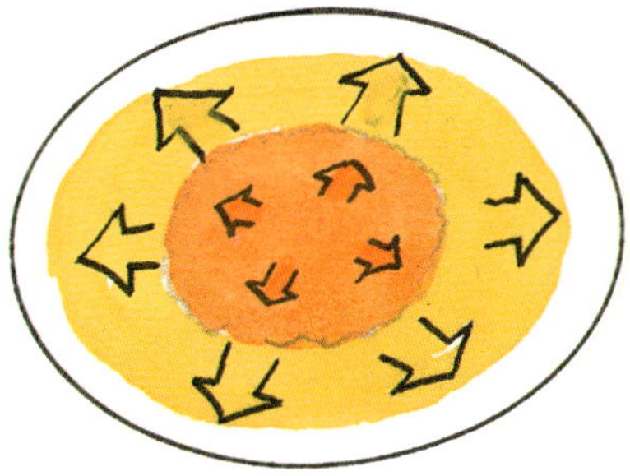

FURTHER IDEAS

Take a long strip of blotting paper. Draw a large dot near the bottom. Hang the strip up so the end just dips into a bowl of water. Watch the colours separate as the water rises up the paper.

COLOURED DYES

Today we can buy clothes in an enormous variety of colours. These colours come from modern artificial dyes made from oil. Before the last century people had always used natural dyes made from plants, animals or materials in the ground.

TIE–DYE A HANDKERCHIEF

2 Tie some string round a white cotton handkerchief as tightly as you can.

1 Collect lots of brown onion skins. Ask an adult to boil them in a pan of water for 20 minutes.

3 Soak the tied handkerchief in the onion skin water for five minutes. Use an oven glove to protect yourself.

4 Cut the string from the dyed handkerchief when cool. Peg the handkerchief to the washing line until it is dry.

FURTHER IDEAS
Many vegetables contain different coloured pigments. See what colour beetroot water or spinach water dye fabric.

WHY IT WORKS

Onion skins contain a chemical called a pigment. Boiling brings out the pigment, which in onion skin is yellow. Compare how well the pigment dyes fabrics other than cotton.

COLOUR CHANGES

Lemons taste sour because they contain acid ("acid" means sour). Hundreds of chemicals are acid. It would be very dangerous if scientists had to taste chemicals to identify them. Instead they use a chemical which changes colour when acid is added.

TESTING FOR ACIDS

1 Ask an adult to chop up half a red cabbage. Boil the chopped cabbage in a pan of water for about five minutes.

2 Remove the cabbage from the water. Cut blotting paper or filter paper into strips.

3 Dip each strip into the cabbage water. Allow the strips to soak the water up.

4 Let the strips dry. When dry try adding drops of vinager, lemon, soap and other harmless substances to each strip.

WHY IT WORKS

Red cabbage contains a chemical called an indicator. Indicators change colour when an acid or alkali is added. Red cabbage juice turns red in acids and green in alkalis. Litmus is an important indicator commonly used by scientists.

FURTHER IDEAS
You can use geranium petals instead of red cabbage. Geranium petals also contain an indicator that changes colour when an acid or alkali is added.

5 Note the different colours you see on each strip.

FANTASTIC LIGHT FACTS

The Sun is 149 million km from the Earth. But because light travels at an amazing 300 million metres per second, it takes only eight minutes for the Sun's light to reach us.

The ancient Greeks believed that the sun was driven form east to west in a flaming chariot, guided by the sun god Helios.

A peacock's bright feathers are created by light reflecting off microscopic fringes called barbules, on each feather.

The world's first photograph was taken in 1826 by a French inventor called Nicéphore Necpce. He captured the view through his window. But the picture took eight hours to take!

The brightest artificial light was produced in 1987 by a laser at the Los Alamos National Laboratory in the United States. The laser was several million times brighter than the Sun.

The longest lasting light bulb can be found in Livermore, California. It was first switched on in 1901.

In a desert, people sometimes think they can see objects or a pool of water in the distance. This is really an image called a mirage. Mirages happen when air near the ground is much hotter than air higher up. As light from the sun passes from cooler to warmer air, it travels faster and is bent upward so that images appear where there is nothing.

Inside our eyes we have light-sensitive cells called cones. These recognise different coloured light. The eye of someone with normal colour vision has three types of cones. One type recognises red light, one blue and the third green light. A colour-blind person will have one or more type of cones missing. To them certain colours, such as red and green, will look the same.

GLOSSARY

Acid
A liquid that turns blue litmus (an indicator) red.

Alkali
A liquid that turns red litmus (an indicator) blue.

Chlorophyll
Chemical pigment that gives green plants their colour. It traps the energy contained in sunlight needed for photosynthesis.

Image
The "picture" of an object usually formed by a lens or photograph.

Indicator
A chemical that changes colour when an acid or alkali is added.

Light ray
A very narrow beam of light.

Litmus
An indicator that turns red in acids and blue in alkalis.

Photosynthesis
A chemical process where light energy trapped by chlorophyll combines with water and air to help make the plant grow.

Pigment
The substance added to paints and dyes to give them their colour.

Primary colour
There are three primary colours of paint and dyes, from which all other colours are made: red, yellow and blue.

Prism
A transparent wedge, usually of glass used to split white light into the colours of the rainbow.

Reflect
When light or sound is bounced back from a surface.

Shadow
Place of darkness created by an object blocking light.

INDEX